A Little Caribbean Cookbook

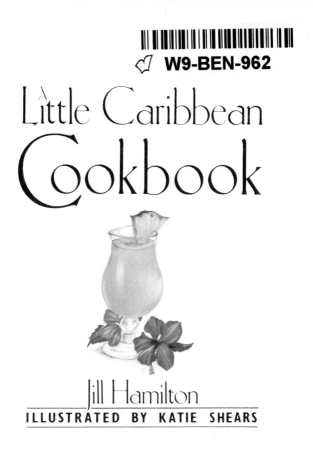

Jill Hamilton

ILLUSTRATED BY KATIE SHEARS

First published in 1990 by
The Appletree Press Ltd
19–21 Alfred Street
Belfast BT2 8DL
Tel. +44 232 243074 Fax +44 232 246756
Text © Jill Hamilton, 1990.
Illustrations © Katie Shears, 1990.

First published in the United States in 1990 by
Chronicle Books, 275 Fifth Street,
San Francisco, California 94103

ISBN 0-87701-685-2

9 8 7 6 5 4 3

A note on measures

Recipes are for four unless otherwise indicated. Spoon
and dry cup measures are level unless otherwise stated.

Introduction

Caribbean cuisine is a delicious melting pot, drawing ingredients and cooking methods from Europe, Africa, Asia, and the Americas, and combining them with the native foods of the islands. Caribbean cooks have absorbed these influences in a unique way, creating their own culinary art over the centuries. Although each island has its specialties, many dishes are found throughout the islands and will often have different names on different islands. Recipes may also vary from island to island, as they do from kitchen to kitchen, but the common denominator in Caribbean cooking is the use of fresh herbs and spices. Seasonings are essential to the sunny cuisine of the Caribbean, and the liberal (yet judicious) use of seasonings can often make the difference between a good dish and a scrumptious dish.

Similarly, hot peppers (chillies/capsicums), are frequently used for flavor and/or heat but, when used too generously, can be disastrously fiery. Peppers come in many varieties, but a good guide is the redder they are, the hotter they are. Peppers are used whole for stews, fricassées, etc., but can also be used chopped with the seeds removed. Please use gloves or a knife and fork when preparing them. Also, be sure to protect your eyes.

The following concoction is considered a basic seasoning:

1 medium onion, chopped	sprig each of parsley, thyme,
1 clove garlic, minced	marjoram
3 blades shallots/chives, including	1/4 tsp allspice
some green tops	1/2 tsp salt
small piece hot pepper,	freshly ground black pepper
deseeded, chopped	dash of Worcestershire sauce

Chop first 5 ingredients very fine and mix together with spices. The mixture will keep, in a sealed container in the refrigerator, for weeks. The seasoning is used to rub into fish, poultry and meat. Incisions may be made in the food and seasoning inserted, to enable the flavors to penetrate deeper.

An old-time method of adding flavor to food in the Caribbean is that of using either burned sugar (caramel), or rubbing sugar directly onto it before the browning process begins. Gravy mix is now available commercially, so most cooks do not go to the trouble of making their own.

For many, the tantalizing aroma produced by this technique brings back childhood memories of when all the mouth-watering dishes were prepared in a buck pot, known by some as a black pot, on a wood and coal stove or coal pot – before the days of electricity or gas of course!

Originally the word Creole referred to people of European descent born in the West Indies. Today, however, it is more often applied to the cuisine of the region and Caribbean Creole cookery is steadily making its mark wherever cooking is an important feature of daily living.

Sop Biscuits

This is a good "filler-upper" at breakfast time for those ravenous appetites so often found in youngsters especially at the seaside where they may have been up since dawn playing on the beach, surfing or collecting shells along the high water mark.

For this quick and simple meal, hard-boil an egg, discard the shell, then slice it neatly in half and put to one side. Place six large plain biscuits around the bottom and sides of a colander. Slowly pour boiling water (you will need a kettleful) over them until softened and transfer biscuits to a heated plate. Spread with butter, sprinkle with salt and pepper to taste and decorate with the egg slices.

The biscuits cool very quickly so you must work fast to get them to table while still hot.

Johnny Bakes

Perhaps these may best be described as similar to a scone – a creole scone. They are popular throughout the Caribbean islands and are baked or fried. "Bakes" are served at any meal and, as their alternative name, Journey Cakes, indicates, are popular for picnics or on jobs where a snack meal is necessary.

---

2 cups flour
1/2 tsp salt
2 tsp baking powder
2 tsp sugar
2 tbsp lard or butter
2/3 cup milk

Sift dry ingredients into bowl, then rub in the fat until mixture resembles breadcrumbs. Pour the milk in and stir to make a soft dough. Knead on a floured board then refrigerate for 30 minutes. Break dough into lemon-sized pieces, roll into balls and flatten to 1/2 inch thickness. Fry these in hot oil until golden or bake in a hot oven at 425°F. While still hot tear bakes open and butter generously.

Coconut Crisps

These snacks are very popular and often served with drinks prior to lunch or dinner. It is important to purchase your mature, brown coconut carefully. Choose one that is dark in color and shake it to ensure it contains liquid. Check the "eyes" at the top; they should be dry and not moldy.

Now, pierce the "eyes" of the coconut with an ice pick or skewer, drain the liquid and reserve it for later use. Bake the coconut in a preheated oven at 400°F for 15 minutes then break it with a hammer and remove the flesh from the shell, levering it out carefully with the point of a strong knife.

Peel off the brown membrane and slice the flesh into thin pieces with a potato peeler. Place these on a baking sheet, in a single layer, sprinkle with salt and bake for 20 minutes in a preheated oven at 350°F.

You may also lightly fry them in deep fat, drain, and then sprinkle with salt.

Brule Johl

This dish is thought to have originated in Trinidad. There are several variations to the spelling but I believe mine to be the colloquial patois pronunciation of "brule gueule", meaning burned mouth/throat. Brule johl is best known as an hors d'oeuvres and served with plain biscuits but is also delicious served in half an avocado from which the seed has been removed but the skin left on.

---

1 lb good quality salt fish,
soaked in water overnight
2 medium onions, finely chopped
about 2 tbsp olive oil
squeeze of fresh lime juice
2 small sweet peppers, green and red, diced
2 tsp hot sauce or 1 small hot pepper, deseeded and chopped

Flake the fish into a bowl, removing bones, skin, and dark flesh. Mix in the onion, olive oil, lime juice, sweet peppers, and hot sauce. Stir well and taste for adjustment in seasonings. Cover tightly and refrigerate, stirring occasionally so that the flavors blend. This will last for several days.

Breadfruit Vichyssoise

Captain Bligh brought the original breadfruit plants to the Caribbean at the end of the eighteenth century. Since then they have become an important staple food.

Despite its name breadfruit is not used as a fruit, but is in fact a very versatile, starchy vegetable. White or sweet potatoes may be substituted.

---

2 tbsp butter or margarine
3 medium onions, finely chopped
1 clove garlic, finely minced
8 oz breadfruit, peeled, decored, and diced (or canned)
1/4 tsp hot pepper, deseeded and chopped (optional)
3 1/4 cups chicken stock
salt and freshly ground black pepper to taste
1 cup light cream or yogurt
1 heaping tbsp shallots/chives, chopped

Melt the butter in a heavy-bottomed saucepan and sauté onions and garlic until transparent. Add remaining ingredients, except cream and shallots. Cover and simmer until the breadfruit is tender. Cool, put into a blender, add the cream and process until smooth, adjusting the seasonings if necessary. Refrigerate until thoroughly chilled. Serve in chilled bowls and decorate with the shallots.

Callaloo Soup

This is probably the best known of all soups in the Caribbean. The main ingredients are taro leaves – often called dasheen – and okras, both originally brought to the region from Africa in the seventeenth century.

I lb callaloo leaves, or spinach as substitute
6 cups chicken stock
I large onion, finely chopped
1/2 lb salt beef, chopped
freshly ground black pepper
4 shallots/chives, using green and white parts, chopped
1/4 tsp thyme
I whole chilli (optional)
12 young okras or 10 oz package
1/2 lb crab meat

Remove the thick stems of the callaloo leaves, chop roughly, and put into a large saucepan with all the ingredients except okras and crab. Cover and simmer until meat is tender. Add the okras, cook for 8 minutes, remove pepper, and blend. Add crab, reheat, and adjust seasonings. Serve piping hot with slices of avocado pear and hot bread.

Pumpkin and Split Pea Soup

The ingredients for this popular and nourishing soup are available all year round. It may also may be made in advance and stored in the deep freeze.

---

1 lb yellow split peas
4 large onions, sliced
4 tbsp butter or margarine
6 cups chicken stock
1 lb pumpkin, peeled and diced
1 lb salt beef, fat removed, diced
piece of fresh chilli, chopped
few dashes of aromatic bitters
freshly ground nutmeg

Rinse and pick over the peas and soak overnight in clear water. Sauté the onions in butter in a large, heavy-bottomed saucepan then add the remaining ingredients. Cover and simmer for about 1 1/2 hours or until peas soften. Allow the soup to cool and then purée in a blender. Adjust the seasoning and reheat before serving with a little nutmeg sprinkled on top.

Spinners / Dumplings

Served with soup these are all-time favorites for young and old alike – in homes both humble and grand. Recipes are myriad, resulting in light, heavy, sweet and not-so-sweet, concoctions. They are sometimes made with cornmeal in addition to flour.

$^1/_4$ cup margarine
1 egg yolk
$^3/_4$ cup flour
salt and pepper
1 egg white, stiffly beaten

Cream the margarine until soft and then beat in the egg yolk. Gradually stir in the flour, egg white, and salt and pepper to taste. Shape into small balls, drop into boiling, salted water and simmer, with the lid on, for 5 minutes. Do not allow them to boil fast. When the dumplings are cooked, drain them and add to the hot soup.

Fried Flying Fish

Barbados has always been famous as the home of flying fish. However they are also found elsewhere in the Caribbean and today these delicacies are exported to other parts of the world.

This is an intricate fish to bone and fillet so I suggest you buy them ready-prepared.

---

juice of 2 medium limes
1 tbsp salt
1 cup water
6 flying fish, filleted
1 small onion, chopped very fine
salt and white pepper
dash of aromatic bitters
2 blades green shallots, sprig each of thyme
and marjoram, chopped very fine
1 egg, beaten lightly with 1 tbsp rum
breadcrumbs
oil or lard for frying

Make a brine with the lime juice, salt, and water, and soak the fish for 15 minutes. Rinse and dry. Mix the seasonings well and press firmly into spaces where bones have been removed. Dip each fish, both sides, into the egg then coat with breadcrumbs. Fry in hot oil or lard, filleted side down first, for 2–3 minutes each side.

Salt Fish Cakes

Salted cod fish – sometimes called bacalau – is known locally as salt fish. It used to be an important source of protein for many but more recently it has become expensive and is widely considered a delicacy. Of the several types available, "box fish" is the least tedious to prepare.

---

8 oz salt fish
6 medium potatoes, peeled
1 egg, beaten
$^1/_2$ tsp chilli, finely chopped
4 tbsp onion, finely chopped
2 tbsp shallots, finely chopped
1 tbsp parsley, finely chopped
2 tbsp butter

Soak the fish in water overnight, then simmer in fresh water for about 20 minutes. Discard all bones and skin and flake very fine. Boil potatoes until tender and crush; mix with remaining ingredients. Shape into cakes and fry in hot fat until golden all over.

To serve as hors d'oeuvres, measure by teaspoon for dropping the mixture into the fat. These may be half cooked, drained, frozen and then heated quickly in hot fat or in the oven.

Okra Stew with Shrimp

This is a delectable spicy creole concoction and so easy to prepare. They're great for a party! Be sure to purchase young, tender okras with no blemishes and to discard the tops when slicing.

1 lb medium shrimp, shelled and deveined	1 cup okras, sliced
squeeze of lime juice	3 medium tomatoes, blanched, skinned, and chopped
4 tbsp butter	1 tbsp tomato paste
2 medium sweet green peppers, deseeded and chopped	$1/4$ tsp thyme
6 tbsp shallots/chives, chopped	1 bay leaf
1 cup corn kernels, fresh, canned or frozen	salt and pepper to taste
	1 whole chilli pepper

Squeeze the lime juice over the shrimp. Heat butter in a frying pan and sauté the green pepper with shallots/chives for 2–3 minutes. Mix in remaining ingredients, except shrimp, and simmer for 10 minutes. Add the shrimp, return to a boil and simmer for a further 5 minutes. Remove bay leaf and chilli before serving.

Ackee and Salt Fish

Known as the national dish of Jamaica, this is served as an hors d'oeuvres or main course and is an intriguing combination of both sharp and bland flavors.

---

1 lb salt fish, soaked overnight
2 tbsp butter
6 rashers bacon, diced
1 large onion, chopped fine
1 clove garlic, minced fine
3 medium tomatoes, blanched, peeled, and chopped
1 tsp fresh chilli, deseeded and chopped fine
freshly ground black pepper
pinch of thyme
salt to taste
2 x 12 oz cans ackee, thoroughly drained

Simmer fish until tender, drain thoroughly, discard skin and bones then flake. Heat the butter, cook bacon until crisp and put aside. Sauté the onion, garlic, tomatoes, chilli, pepper, and thyme for 5 minutes, stirring well. Mix in the fish, ackee, and bacon and continue to cook for a few minutes until heated through. Serve with Johnny Bakes (see page 9), Fried Plantain (see page 34), or Rice and Peas (see page 37).

Pepperpot

Devised as a means to preserve surplus meat from hunting forays, Pepperpot is a legacy from the Arawak indians. Pepperpot is considered a "treat" throughout the Caribbean.

---

4 lb beef
4 lb fatty pork
1 old chicken
1 whole oxtail
4 tsp salt
4 tbsp brown sugar
muslin bag of 3 tbsp whole cloves
muslin bag of 6 whole chillies
8 tbsp cassareep

Cut meat into large-ish pieces. Put into pan (preferably earthenware or stainless steel), cover with cold water, add salt, and simmer until tender. Add remaining ingredients and cook until meat falls off the bones. (Tie the bags of cloves and peppers to saucepan handle so as they don't find themselves on someone's plate!) Serve with rice or boiled and sliced sweet potatoes.

If brought to a boil daily, pepperpot keeps almost indefinitely. Cooked meats (no rabbit, lamb/mutton, fish or vegetables) may be added with additional water and cassareep. Pepperpot can be frozen and reheated.

Creole Chicken

This flavorsome dish provides a hearty main course for lunch, dinner, or a picnic. Serve with local sweet potatoes, either baked or crushed.

---

4 lb chicken, jointed or legs and thighs
brown sugar
hot oil for frying
4 medium onions, chopped
2 cloves garlic, minced
3 medium sweet peppers, deseeded and chopped
8 oz tomato paste
1 cup seedless raisins
1 tbsp curry powder
2 cups chicken stock
1 bay leaf
salt and pepper to taste
1 tbsp parsley, chopped

Pat dry the chicken pieces. Rub chicken with brown sugar and fry quickly – the sugar must not burn. When browned, remove to an oven-proof dish. Cook onions and garlic in oil until soft. Add remaining ingredients and simmer for about 5 minutes. Pour sauce over chicken, cover and bake for 45 minutes at 350°F. Remove cover and cook for a further 30 minutes or until tender.

Fried Plaintain

Although a fruit, plantain is used as a vegetable and must be cooked to make it palatable. It looks rather like a banana but usually has a more pointed end. It may be boiled, baked, or fried. Sliced crosswise and fried it makes a delectable cocktail snack.

---

2 ripe plantains, peeled
oil for frying

Cut the plantains lengthwise into thin slices. Heat the oil in a frying pan and fry the slices until golden brown, turning once – about 2 minutes on each side. Drain on absorbent paper. If preferred, the plantains may be sliced crosswise. Serve with fish, roast chicken, or pork, in fact whatever you fancy.

Another delicious method of preparation is to cut each plantain lengthwise, into 2 or 3 pieces, wrap individually in bacon, secure with a toothpick, and bake until bacon is crisp.

Rice and Peas

There are endless recipes for this dish, varying from household to household. Sometimes beans (e.g. red or black) are substituted for peas. If fresh peas are not available use half the quantity of dried peas and prepare according to instructions on the package.

---

4 cups water
1 cup pigeon or black-eyed peas
1 1/2 tsp salt
1 cup rice
1 medium onion, chopped
2 tbsp butter or margarine

Bring the water to a rapid boil and then add the peas and salt. Cover, reduce heat, and simmer for 45 minutes. Stir in the rice, onion, and butter, mixing well. Cover and simmer until the water is absorbed — about 20 minutes. Fluff with a fork and serve immediately. Rice and Peas goes equally well with fish, chicken, meat and Pepperpot (see page 30).

"Turned" Corn Cou-Cou

Traditionally, this cornmeal dish is served as an accompaniment to chicken, meat, and fish, particularly flying fish. Serve it with a knob of melting butter on the top or with a rich gravy.

---

1 ½ cups cornmeal
1 ¼ cups cold water
8 young okras, thinly sliced
2 ½ cups boiling water
1 tsp salt
knob of butter or rich gravy

Mix the cornmeal and cold water to a smooth paste and put aside. Cook the okras in boiling water for 5 minutes. Lower heat, add salt and cornmeal, stirring continuously with a cou-cou stick (or wooden spoon), until mixture is fairly stiff. When it breaks cleanly from sides of saucepan the cou-cou is ready. Butter a bowl, turn mixture into it, shaking the mixture so that it takes the shape of the bowl. Turn onto serving dish and with the back of a spoon, make an indentation in the top and place butter or gravy in it.

West Indian Christophene Salad

This pear-shaped vegetable is also known as cho-cho or chayote. It may be eaten raw or cooked, but be careful not to overcook it.

2 tsp mustard
2 tbsp red wine vinegar
6 tbsp olive oil
2 tsp garlic, finely minced
1/4 tsp dried hot pepper flakes
salt and pepper to taste
2 lb christophene, peeled and seed removed
1 lb tomatoes, sliced
3 small onions, thinly sliced
2 tbsp parsley, finely chopped

Make a dressing with the first six ingredients. Put aside. Cut the christophene into strips and steam for 3–4 minutes. Cool, then arrange on platter with the tomatoes and onions. Sprinkle the parsley on top. Cover with plastic wrap, chill for a few hours, and serve with the dressing.

Calypso Dressing

Avocado pear, known also as zaboca or alligator pear, is a fruit. It is frequently used in salads, dips, and dressings and makes a delicious soup. The following recipe is versatile – try it as a dip with crudités such as sweet red pepper chunks and carrot sticks to give a color contrast.

I large ripe avocado, peeled
6 tbsp thick mayonnaise
3 tsp lemon juice
2 tsp tarragon vinegar
couple dashes aromatic bitters
$^1/_4$ tsp pepper sauce
I tsp Worcestershire sauce
2 level tsp parsley, finely chopped
2 level tsp shallots/chives, finely chopped
salt and freshly ground black pepper to taste

Crush the avocado with a stainless steel fork, or purée in blender. Add remaining ingredients and adjust seasonings.

To test an avocado for ripeness, press the center of the bottom – it should "give" slightly. Do not shake it because if the seed is loose it will damage the flesh.

Banana Fritters

Bananas are one of the more easily obtainable fruits in Caribbean markets. They are most nutritious but also very high in calories. To be thoroughly ripe they should have some brown spots on the skin.

---

6 ripe bananas
1 tbsp sugar
pinch of grated nutmeg
1 egg, well-beaten
²/₃ cup milk
flour
pinch of baking soda
fat for frying
fine sugar

Peel and crush the bananas to a pulp. Add the sugar, nutmeg, and egg. Stir well and add the milk and enough flour to make a batter with a consistency for frying. Add the baking soda while stirring. Drop spoonfuls of the mixture into boiling fat and fry on both sides for a few minutes. Serve hot with a little fine sugar sprinkled over them.

Rum Omelette

This is a simple but elegant finale to any good meal. Brought flaming to the table it will be a conversation dish. A good quality 5-year-old rum should be used.

4 eggs
fat for frying
guava jelly
rum, about 2 tbsp per omelette

Allow 1 egg for each person. Beat lightly and pour into boiling fat in a frying pan. Spread as thinly as possible without breaking or damaging the omelette. Allow the bottom to become golden brown then remove carefully from the pan and drain well. Now spread some jelly on the inside, roll up like a sausage and place on hot dish.

To serve, drain the fat from the frying pan, pour in the rum, heat, and ignite. Pour this over the omelettes and serve immediately.

Mango and Banana Pudding

A tropical variation of the traditional crumble. Other fruits such as guava, mammee apple, and paw paw (papaya) may be used. Serve hot or cold with vanilla ice-cream or fresh coconut milk.

---

2 medium mangoes, peeled
1 tsp lime juice
4 tbsp rum
few dashes aromatic bitters
3/4 cup flour
pinch of salt
1/2 cup brown sugar
1/2 cup butter
5 medium, ripe but firm bananas, sliced

Slice the mango flesh into bite-sized pieces. Mix the lime juice, rum and bitters together. In a separate bowl, sift together the flour and salt, add the sugar, then cut in the butter until mixture is crumbly. Put aside. In a greased oven-proof dish, layer the fruit, starting and finishing with banana. Drizzle each layer with the rum mixture. Now sprinkle the crumble over the bananas and press down lightly. Bake in a preheated oven at 350°F until the top is lightly-browned.

Coconut Bread

Although generous with its calories this is a favorite, whether sliced and served "as is" or buttered.

---

2 cups sugar
I cup butter
or margarine
2 eggs
I tsp vanilla or almond essence
2–3 cups coconut, grated – use desiccated
if fresh is not available
6 cups flour
2 tsp baking powder
¹/₂ tsp salt
I cup coconut water
I cup seedless raisins
2 tsp sugar

Beat the sugar and butter until light and fluffy. Add eggs, essence, coconut, flour, baking powder, and salt, beating constantly. Mix in the coconut water and raisins, stirring well. Put this mixture into a greased loaf pan and sprinkle sugar on the top. Bake in a preheated oven at 325°F for 40–45 minutes, until it is golden brown on top.

Rum · Rum Cocktail

Rum be sweet, rum be sweet,
Doan leh dis drink
Sweep yuh orf yuh feet!

Just as tequila is associated with Mexico or whisky with Scotland so too is rum associated with the Caribbean. No Caribbean cookbook therefore, however small, should be without some information on the national drink!

When rum was first produced in the seventeenth century it was described as "a hot, hellish and terrible liquor" and was known as rumbullion, alias Kill Devil. Today, thanks to modern methods of fermentation and distillation of the sugar cane, followed by the aging process, we have a mellow, pleasant-tasting, golden liquid which has earned worldwide fame. There are many brands, varying in flavor, for you to sample.

There is also white rum, clear and strong-tasting. This is popular with many, especially those who appreciate minimal "after effects" following overindulgence! As with dark and light rums it is used with mixes, etc.

Rum Cocktail The following is probably the most simple and the most traditional rum cocktail in the Caribbean islands. Before World War II long drinks with mixes were seldom called for. Most people who drank spirits drank cocktails or short "snaps".

---

one good measure rum
2 dashes aromatic bitters
few drops sugar syrup (optional)
3–4 ice cubes well-crushed

Shake all the ingredients very thoroughly in a cocktail shaker or, if that is not available, in a strong bottle. The shaking will produce a good frothy "head" when the drink is poured into the glass. This cocktail should be consumed before the "head" disperses. Do not let it get tepid.

Sugar Syrup

---

2 cups sugar
2 ½ cups water

Mix the sugar and water together in a saucepan over a medium heat. Stir constantly until sugar has dissolved. Cool, bottle, and refrigerate until required. This syrup is good for all drinks.

Planter's Punch

The drink known as punch has been made for many centuries. In its simplest form it is rum and water, served hot or cold, with sugar syrup added and fresh lime juice.
There is a little rhyme which goes:

one of sour	*pure lime juice*
two of sweet	*sugar syrup*
three of strong, and	*rum*
four of weak	*water and ice*

To those basic ingredients add several dashes of aromatic bitters, then stir and pour over crushed ice, adding some grated nutmeg on the top. Decorate the glass with chunks of pineapple etc., and place a hibiscus flower at the side to give it some tropical charm!

Medicinal Rum

This cure for a "head" (common) cold has been handed down for generations. Consume it as hot as possible when already in bed and be prepared to perspire profusely!

In a ceramic mug place 1 teaspoon brown sugar, 2 cloves, 1 measure fresh lime juice, a small stick of cinnamon, and 2 measures of rum. Stir until sugar is dissolved and then add boiling water to taste – about 4 measures.

Index